34880000823505

**BOOK CHARGING CARD**

979.5

Accession No. _____ Call No. WIN

Author Winans, Jay D. _____

Title Oregon _____

Date

979.5
WIN

Winans, Jay D.
Oregon

34880000823505

# OREGON

**Jay D. Winans**

Published by Weigl Publishers Inc.
123 South Broad Street, Box 227
Mankato, MN   56002
USA
Web site: http://www.weigl.com

Library of Congress Cataloging-in-Publication Data available upon
request from the publisher. Fax: (507) 388-2746 for the attention of the
Publishing Records Department.

ISBN  1-59036-002-8

Printed in the United States of America
1 2 3 4 5 6 7 8 9 10    05 04 03 02 01

**Editor**
Michael Lowry
**Copy Editor**
Diana Marshall
**Designers**
Warren Clark
Terry Paulhus
**Photo Researcher**
Angela Lowen

**Photograph Credits**
Every reasonable effort has been made to trace ownership and to obtain
permission to reprint copyright material. The publishers would be
pleased to have any errors or omissions brought to their attention so
that they may be corrected in subsequent printings.

**Cover:** Main (Corel Corporation), Background (Corel Corporation);
**Corbis Corporation:** pages 3B, 13T, 15T, 15B, 26B; **Corel Corporation:** pages 3T, 3M,
5BL, 5T, 8T, 8B, 9T, 9B, 10T, 10B, 11T, 11B, 13B, 14T, 14B, 19B, 21T, 26T, 28T, 29B;
**David Falconer:** pages 4T, 4B, 6, 7T, 7B, 12T, 12B, 20BL, 20BR, 22T; **Donna
Ikenberry:** pages 16B, 20T; **Bruce Leighty:** page 21B; **Oregon Historical Society:**
pages 16T, 17T, 17B, 18T, 18B, 19T; **PhotoDisc Corporation:** pages 27T, 27B, 28R;
**Photofest:** pages 24T, 25T, 25B; **Bob Pool:** pages 22B, 23T, 23BR, 24B.

# CONTENTS

**Reaching heights of over 10,000 feet, Oregon's mountains are an impressive sight.**

# INTRODUCTION

Located in the beautiful Pacific Northwest, Oregon has been attracting visitors for centuries. In the mid-1800s, more than 500,000 pioneers followed the Oregon Trail from Independence, Missouri, to Oregon's fertile Willamette Valley. These early settlers were attracted to the state's abundant supply of furs, its fertile land, and its rich forests. Their journey is known as the "great **migration**."

No one knows for sure where the name Oregon came from. It is believed that early French settlers once called the mighty Columbia River, the River of Storms, or *ouragan*, which means hurricane. Today, the state's stunning combination of mountains, forest, and coastline have led many to refer to Oregon as the "Pacific Wonderland."

## QUICK FACTS

**Salem was established** as the capital of Oregon in 1854.

**Oregon's birthday is** on St. Valentine's Day, February 14, 1859.

**Oregon is nicknamed** "The Beaver State." The beaver was an important source of income for early trappers in Oregon.

**The Pacific Northwest** is a region in the northwestern United States along the Pacific coast. It includes the states of Washington and Oregon, as well as parts of northern California, western Canada, and southern Alaska.

**Portland's Japanese Garden is considered to be one of the most beautiful gardens of its kind outside of Japan.**

**Oregon was the first state to complete its part of the interstate freeway system in 1966.**

# Getting There

Oregon's western border follows the Pacific coast. The state is bordered by Washington to the north, Idaho to the east, and California and Nevada to the south. The Columbia River forms most of the border dividing Oregon from Washington, and the Snake River forms a large section of the border dividing Oregon from Idaho.

Oregon's road network is immense. The state's 97,000-square-mile area is covered by 123,000 miles of roads and highways. The replacement cost of the pavement alone would be more than $60 billion.

Portland International Airport is the largest of sixteen commercial-passenger airports in Oregon. The airline industry is an important part of Oregon's economy as Portland and other airports serve as gateways to Asia.

## QUICK FACTS

**Nine lighthouses are** found on the Oregon coastline, but only five of them are still used to alert boats.

**Oregon has the** only state flag with a different image on each side. On the front side, the words, "State of Oregon," are written in gold across the top of the flag. On the back side, a gold beaver is pictured on a field of navy blue.

**Front Side of Oregon Flag**

### Oregon Location Map

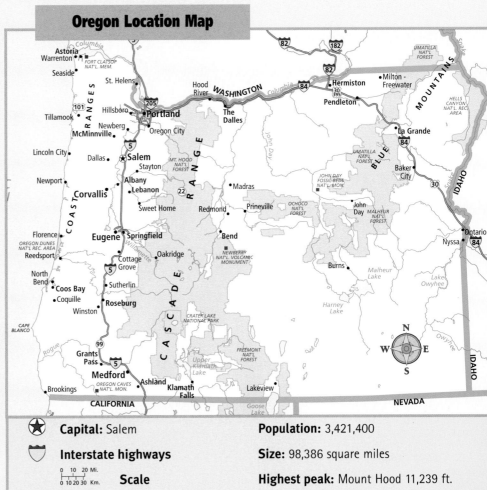

**Capital:** Salem

**Interstate highways**

Scale
0 10 20 Mi.
0 10 20 30 Km.

**Population:** 3,421,400

**Size:** 98,386 square miles

**Highest peak:** Mount Hood 11,239 ft.

Spanish explorers first sailed the coastal waters off Oregon in 1543. Eventually, many European nations were drawn to the area for its wealth of fur-bearing animals and their valuable pelts. Following the **Louisiana Purchase**, in 1803, United States President Thomas Jefferson sent Meriwether Lewis and William Clark to explore the North American continent west of the Mississippi River. Their successful expedition to the Oregon coast encouraged trappers and settlers to journey to Oregon throughout the nineteenth century.

With the European settlers came European diseases, which resulted in the deaths of many Native Americans. Competition between the settlers and the Native Americans over valuable land and natural resources often developed into violent conflicts. Wars among the Native-American groups and with the settlers almost wiped out the Native Americans in the region. Those who survived were forced to live on reservations. In 1859, Oregon became the thirty-third state of the United States, and the logging and farming industries fueled the new economy.

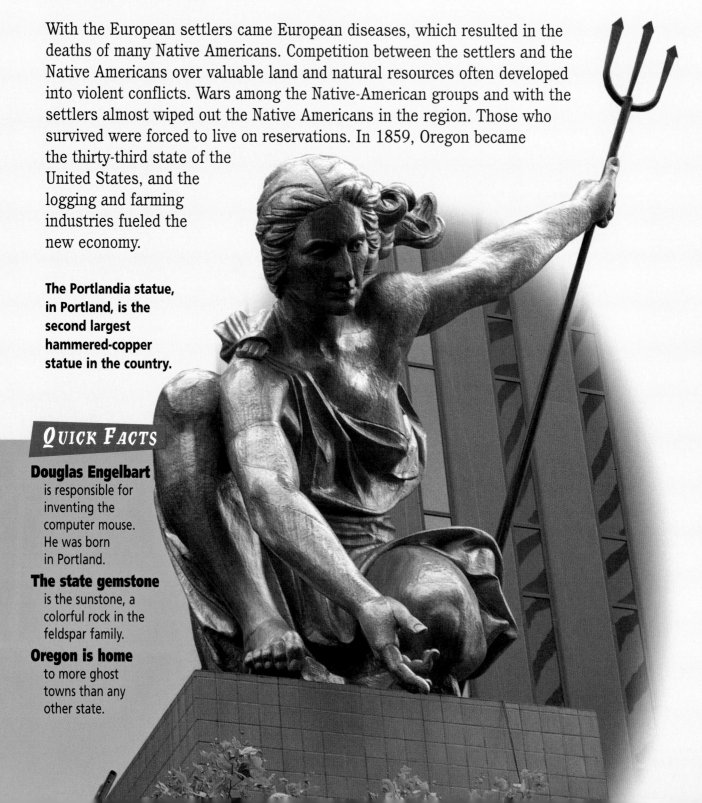

**The Portlandia statue, in Portland, is the second largest hammered-copper statue in the country.**

### QUICK FACTS

**Douglas Engelbart** is responsible for inventing the computer mouse. He was born in Portland.

**The state gemstone** is the sunstone, a colorful rock in the feldspar family.

**Oregon is home** to more ghost towns than any other state.

**The Oregon Plan was developed to restore salmon and trout populations in the state.**

During the last half of the twentieth century, many of Oregon's traditional industries, such as forestry and fishing, came under attack. Over-fishing of salmon and over-logging of national forests led to a severe decline of these resources. Environmental protection laws were created to protect the state's natural resources. Despite sawmill and paper plant closures, fishing limits, and a shrinking rural population, Oregonians were quick to recover. New high-technology industries, such as electronics, have strengthened the economy and allowed the state to thrive.

Oregon is a haven for outdoor recreation. The mountains and coastline provide a wealth of opportunity for activities such as swimming, skiing, boating, hunting, fishing, and windsurfing. In fact, the Columbia River Gorge in northern Oregon is known as "the windsurfing capital of the world." Today, Oregon's friendly population and diversified economy attract people from all over the world.

## QUICK FACTS

**In 1993,** Oregon was the first and is still one of the few states to allow voters to cast their ballots by mail.

**In 1998,** Oregon raised its hourly minimum wage to the highest in the country.

**At 620 feet,** Multnomah Falls is the second highest waterfall in the United States.

**Oregon's motto is** *Alis Volat Propiis,* a Latin phrase meaning, "She Flies With Her Own Wings."

**The state song** is "Oregon, My Oregon," by J. A. Buchanan and Henry Murtagh.

**Oregon has nearly 300 miles of coastline.**

# LAND AND CLIMATE

**Oregon's coastal mountain range runs parallel to the coast.**

Oregon has a varied landscape, which stretches from the Pacific Ocean to the Blue Mountains in the northeast. The mountain ranges are very high, with numerous peaks over 10,000 feet, while Hells Canyon, the deepest canyon in the United States, is more than 8,000 feet deep. The western third of the state is mountainous and lush with dense rain forests. The eastern part of the state is characterized by arid deserts. Oregon's coastline is made up largely of steep cliffs. Columbia River is Oregon's major river, and its main tributary is the Snake River.

The coastal regions enjoy a mild climate, with temperatures ranging from freezing to about 45° Fahrenheit in January. In summer, coastal temperatures average 60°F in July. Average temperatures in the east are more extreme and dip as low as 25°F in January. They rise to between 60°F to 90°F in July.

## QUICK FACTS

**Mount Hood,** an old volcano, is the highest point in Oregon, at 11,235 feet. The lowest point is sea level, at the Pacific Ocean.

**The Metasequoia,** an early relative of the redwood, was a tree that grew in great numbers millions of years ago in Oregon. Fossils of this huge tree are found around ancient lake beds. Amazingly, three living Metasequoia trees were discovered in China in 1941.

**At 1,932 feet,** Crater Lake is the deepest lake in the United States and the seventh deepest lake in the world.

**Crater Lake National Park, in southwestern Oregon, is known for its incredible views and for the intense blue color of the lake's water.**

Oregon's forests have trees that are over 120 feet tall.

# NATURAL RESOURCES

One of Oregon's greatest resources is its high-quality Jory soil, which is named after an early pioneer family. More than 300,000 acres of Jory soil can be found in the rolling hills around the Willamette Valley. These deep, well-drained soils are excellent for agriculture and forestry.

Forests are found throughout the state. In fact, more than half of Oregon is covered in forests, which mainly consist of Douglas fir, spruce, and other hardwoods. The abundant forests provided the raw materials for Oregon's first major industry—logging.

While much of Oregon is mountainous, the eastern part of the state and the wide valleys between the mountain ranges provide excellent grasslands for cattle grazing and for the production of wheat, alfalfa, barley, and vegetables.

## QUICK FACTS

**Only 10 percent** of Oregon's original old-growth forests remain today.

**The Oregon Natural Resources Council** helped to create the Endangered American Wilderness Act and the Oregon Wilderness Act, which protect more than 1.2 million acres of land in Oregon.

**Gravel, sand, cement,** and pumice are mined in Oregon, and the only domestic **nickel** mine is also found there.

**Jory soil is** the unofficial state soil.

Oregon's Jory soil is used for growing crops such as Christmas trees, grass seeds, and wine grapes.

**In 1995, Oregon created the nation's first state sponsored tree program. It is designed to make the public aware of the importance of Oregon's trees.**

# PLANTS AND ANIMALS

Oregon's landscape is a spectacular combination of old-growth forests and vibrant wildflowers, such as azaleas and Columbia lilies. Cedars, cottonwoods, firs, hemlocks, maples, pines, and spruces all grow in Oregon's forests. Oregon is known for its hardwood forests.

The state tree is the Douglas fir, which was named after William Douglas, a Scottish botanist, who visited the area in 1825. An average height for these gigantic trees is 200 feet with a trunk diameter of 6 feet, but they have been found at 325 feet with a 15-foot diameter. The Douglas fir was the basis for Oregon's extensive logging industry. The tree is said to be a stronger building material than concrete.

## QUICK FACTS

**The state flower** is the Oregon grape, which can be found throughout the state.

**Oregon's state** bird, the western meadowlark, has a beautiful and easily identifiable song.

**The state insect** is the Oregon swallowtail, a yellow butterfly native to the sagebrush canyons of the Columbia and Snake Rivers.

**Zoo Oregon,** in Portland, has the most successful elephant breeding program in the nation.

**The Columbia lily can grow in mountainous regions at elevations of 6,000 feet. It is also known as the tiger lily.**

QUICK FACTS

**The state fish** is the Chinook salmon. It is the largest of the Pacific salmons and is also known as the spring, king, and typee salmon.

**The Seaside Aquarium** established the first program to breed harbor seals in captivity. The aquarium was founded in Seaside in 1937.

**Oregon's first wildlife** protection laws were developed in the 1890s. The laws were intended to protect the declining population of beavers, bobcats, cougars, coyotes, and wolves.

Today, Oregon still has a thriving animal population. The state is home to a variety of large animals, including black bears, bighorn sheep, elk, mule deers, pronghorn antelopes, and white-tail deers. Smaller animals are even more numerous. Bobcats, gray and red foxes, martens, muskrats, minks, raccoons, river otters, badgers, coyotes, opossums, porcupines, beavers, skunks, weasels, and wolverines can all be found in Oregon.

Oregon's coastal waters are home to sea otters and sea lions. Once numerous, salmon, halibut, and other species of fish are now carefully controlled to protect their numbers. Unfortunately, the bull trout has been identified by the U.S. Fish and Wildlife Service as a threatened or endangered species in the Columbia and Klamath Rivers respectively.

**Oregon's sea otters were once hunted to near extinction for their fur. They are now being re-introduced to the area.**

**There are more than 200 elk living in the Jewell Meadows Wildlife Area in Oregon.**

Mount Hood is one of the most-climbed mountains in the world.

# TOURISM

The mountain ranges, canyons, volcanoes, forests, and coastline of Oregon offer abundant recreational opportunities, and attract tourists to the state. Oregonians are careful to balance tourism and environmental protection. The state has 295 miles of protected natural coastline, most of which can be enjoyed by driving along the Pacific Coast Scenic Byway. The route provides travelers with views of beautiful rugged coastline and white sand dunes.

Mountain climbers, rock climbers, and hikers from around the world are drawn to Oregon's numerous mountain ranges. Mount Hood, the tallest of the Cascade Mountains, is a popular destination for mountaineers.

The Pacific Wonderland attracts hikers and campers from around the world.

## QUICK FACTS

**Ranger,** a climbing dog, climbed Mount Hood a total of 500 times. He is buried at the top of the mountain.

**The first wedding** to be held at the top of Mount Hood was in July 1915.

**The Painted Hills,** at the John Day Fossil Beds National Monument, are a popular tourist destination. The stripes of color are the result of layers of volcanic ash.

Oregon supplies about 20 percent of all the saw timber in the United States.

# INDUSTRY

Manufacturing accounts for 18 percent of Oregon's **gross state product**. Despite the severe decline in logging in the 1990s, wood processing is still one of the state's most important industries and employs more than 64,000 people. Lumber products, such as plywood, hardwood, pulp, and paper, are made from the state's Douglas fir, sitka spruce, and ponderosa pine trees. In order to protect animal habitat, shade, and rain forest, tree harvesting in Oregon is done in the most environmentally sensitive manner of any forestry operation in North America.

In the 1990s, high-technology became an important part of Oregon's economy. The manufacturing of electronic and electrical products creates more money for the state than any other industry. High-technology companies such as Tektronix, Hewlett-Packard, and Intel Corporation all have offices in Oregon. Some of the newer industries in Oregon include plastics, **biotechnology**, software, and film and video production.

## QUICK FACTS

**The Oregon metals** industry employs more than 60,000 people.

**Food-processing and** metal-manufacturing are important to Oregon's economy.

**Tektronix,** a major electronics firm, formed in Oregon in 1948.

**Until the 1990s,** no other national forest produced more saw logs than Oregon's Willamette National Forest. One 200,000-acre district in Willamette produced 86 million **board feet** of timber.

**Oregon ranks second** in the country, after Washington, for **hydroelectricity.** Hydroelectric plants generate 81 percent of the state's electricity.

Bonneville Dam, on the Columbia River, is an important source of electricity in Oregon. The dam is 197 feet high and 2,690 feet long.

**Agriculture is responsible for about 3 percent of Oregon's gross state product.**

# GOODS AND SERVICES

There are more than 40,000 farms in Oregon, which contribute about $3.4 billion to the state economy. Oregon is well-known for the diversity of its agriculture. The state's different climate zones and rich soils produce a wide variety of crops, including Christmas trees, hazelnuts, peppermint, orchard fruits, and wine grapes. The sale of crops accounts for nearly three-quarters of the agricultural income, with wheat being the state's leading crop.

Fishing contributes about $76 million to the state economy. Shellfish such as oysters, mussels, clams, shrimp, crabs, and scallops are harvested on the coast. While over-fishing has led to a decline in Oregon's salmon fishing industry, salmon is still the most valuable commercial catch.

**Salmon are an important catch for both commercial and recreational fishers in Oregon.**

**Beef cattle are the most important livestock product in Oregon.**

The service industry dominates Oregon's economy, accounting for 82 percent of the gross state product. The wholesale and retail trade is the most important service industry in the state. It employs more people than any other industry. Other important service industries include banking, government, and real estate.

Education is very important to Oregonians. The state spends more money per student on education than the national average and has one of the highest literacy rates in the country. Oregon is home to a variety of public and private colleges and universities, including the University of Portland, the University of Oregon, and Oregon State University.

Oregonians keep current by reading one of the state's twenty daily newspapers, including the *Oregonian*, the *Register-Guard*, and the *Statesman Journal*. The state is also home to 180 radio stations and 30 television stations.

## QUICK FACTS

**The average citizen** in the United States encounters 250 semiconductors, or computer chips, in a single day, many of which may have been made by one of Oregon's nine semi-conductor manufacturers.

**Linus Carl Pauling,** world-renowned chemist, scientist, and political activist was born in Portland. Pauling attended Oregon Agricultural College, now Oregon State University, in Corvallis. He won the 1954 Nobel Prize for Chemistry and the 1962 Nobel Prize for Peace.

**Oregon has no** self-serve gas stations.

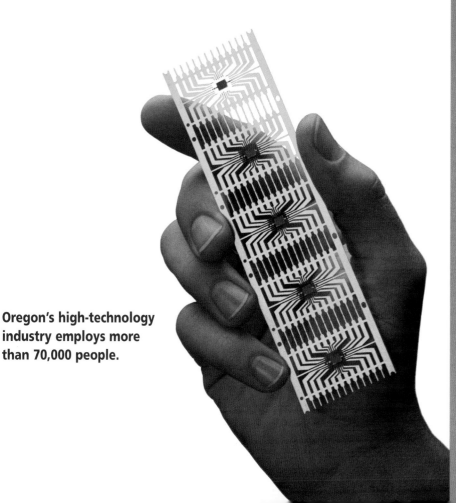

**Oregon's high-technology industry employs more than 70,000 people.**

**The name Yakima means "people of the narrows" or "people of the gap."**

# FIRST NATIONS

When Lewis and Clark arrived in the Oregon area in 1805, they noted in their journals that Oregon was populated by many thousands of Native Americans. Within only a few decades, most of the Native-American groups living in the area had been completely wiped out by disease or war.

Four major Native-American nations lived in the coastal area of Oregon. Each nation was made up of many smaller groups. The Chinookan Nation lived along the Columbia River and the Pacific coast. The Yakonan Nation lived on Coos Bay and the Yaquina, Coquille, and Umpqua Rivers. The Salishan Nation lived on Tillamook Bay and the adjacent rivers in northwest Oregon.

Native Peoples also occupied land in the interior of Oregon. The Shahaptian Nation in northeast Oregon lived between the Rocky Mountains and the Cascade Mountains and included the Nez Perce, Palouse, Wallawalla, and Yakima groups.

**The Oregon Trail Interpretive Center, in Baker City, preserves the history and the culture of the Native Peoples who once lived along the Oregon Trail.**

## QUICK FACTS

**The Salish and** other groups tied boards to their babies' heads to create a flat profile from the top of the head to the tip of the nose.

**The Chinook lived** communally in 40- to 100-foot long houses that were made of planks and were half-submerged in the ground.

**Chinook jargon was** a language invented by trappers and Native Americans so that they could communicate. The language was based on a simplified version of Chinookan, with many European words.

**The Paiute,** also known as the Shoshone, lived in eastern Oregon.

**Captain Robert Gray served in the Continental Navy during the American Revolution.**

# EXPLORERS AND MISSIONARIES

The area that became Oregon attracted the interest of many different nations of Europe. Spanish explorers Juan Cabrillo and Bartolome Ferrelo, seeking the **Northwest Passage**, sailed the coastline in 1542, followed by Martin Aquilar in 1602 and Sebastian Vizcaino in 1603. In 1579, Sir Francis Drake planted the British flag in Oregon's soil, claiming the region on behalf of Queen Elizabeth I. In the late seventeenth century, Russia began exploring the area in search of an abundant source of furs.

In 1792, Captain Robert Gray, a trader from the United States, became the first European to sail into the mouth of the Columbia River. He named the river after his ship, *Columbia*. The United States soon claimed the Pacific Northwest region based on Gray's exploration of the Columbia River.

**Fur trading mogul John Jacob Astor founded Astoria in 1811.**

## QUICK FACTS

**The earliest Europeans** to see the Oregon coast were Spanish sailors returning to Mexico from the Philippines in 1500.

**Neither Captains** James Cook nor George Vancouver, both skilled explorers, could find the opening to the Columbia River.

**In 1789,** Captain Robert Gray became the first person from the United States to travel around the world. He died in poverty in 1806.

**The first Christian** missionaries came to Oregon in the 1830s at the invitation of four Native Americans, all of whom died before the missionaries arrived.

# EARLY SETTLERS

**The Oregon Trail was the most important passage to the west in the mid-1800s.**

Under the terms of the Louisiana Purchase, the United States acquired a vast amount of territory from France. In May 1804, Meriwether Lewis and William Clark left St. Louis, Missouri, to lead an expedition across the lands west of the Mississippi River. They traveled over land across the plains, through the Rocky Mountains, and to the mouth of the Columbia River. In the winter of 1804–1805, Lewis and Clark hired the interpreters Toussaint Charbonneau and his wife, Sacagawea. Sacagawea was an important addition to Lewis and Clark's party as she was able to guide them through the lands of the Shoshones and instruct the explorers on the customs of the Native Peoples they encountered.

The expedition nearly ended in the late summer of 1805 when it met bad weather in the Rocky Mountains and ran out of provisions. The party was saved by a Nez Perce chief, who mapped the safest route through the Rockies for them. The explorers established a camp over the winter of 1805–1806 at the site of what is now Seaside, Oregon, and finally returned to St. Louis in September 1806.

## QUICK FACTS

**A replica of** Lewis and Clark's 1805 winter camp can be seen at the Fort Clatsop National Memorial.

**The Lewis and Clark** expedition covered a total distance of 8,000 miles.

**Sacagawea's name means** "bird woman" in Shoshone.

**Fort Vancouver was the main supply depot for fur trading in the Pacific Northwest.**

**Oregon's early settlers are represented by the statue of an "Oregon Pioneer" atop the Capitol in Salem.**

The first United States settlement in the area was a trading post established in Astoria by John Jacob Astor in 1811. The British captured the trading post during the War of 1812, and the area remained under the control of the **Hudson's Bay Company** until settlers from Europe and the United States began arriving along the Oregon Trail in the 1830s. The pioneers settled in the Willamette River Valley. The earliest settlers logged the forest of the coastal mountain ranges.

An 1846 treaty with England established Oregon Country as part of the United States, with the northern boundary at the forty-ninth parallel. Today, the forty-ninth parallel forms the boundary between the United States and Canada. In 1848, the United States government defined the Oregon Territory as the area from the **Continental Divide** to the coast and from the forty-ninth parallel to the forty-second parallel. When Oregon became a state, in 1859, its present nearly rectangular boundary was established.

## QUICK FACTS

**Gold was discovered** in the Cascade Mountains in 1858, bringing numerous gold miners and other settlers seeking their fortune in Oregon.

**From the 1820s** to the 1870s, numerous small wars were fought between settlers and Native Americans in the Oregon region.

**The most common crops grown by Oregon's early settlers were garden vegetables such as potatoes, cabbage, peas, turnips, onions, parsley, tomatoes, and corn.**

**Oregon is the tenth largest state in land area, yet it only has 1.2 percent of the nation's population.**

# POPULATION

The population of Oregon is approximately 3.4 million people. Two-thirds of Oregon's population lives in the four largest cities—Portland, Eugene, Salem, and Medford. The vast majority of the population lives west of the Cascade Mountains.

Compared to the rest of the United States, Oregon has experienced a population boom. In the 1990s, the population of Oregon increased by more than 20 percent, whereas the population of the United States increased by 13 percent. People in Oregon still have plenty of room compared to the rest of the country. The average number of people per square mile in the nation is just under 80, but in Oregon, the average is about 35 people per square mile.

**Over the next 20 years, Portland is expected to double in size.**

## QUICK FACTS

**Approximately 65 percent** of Oregon families own their own homes.

**About 86 percent** of Oregon's population is of European heritage.

**Portland is Oregon's** largest city, with a population of 529,000 people. Portland is nicknamed "The City of Roses," for its many beautiful parks.

**Built in 1869, Portland's Pioneer Courthouse was the only federal courthouse in Oregon for 58 years.**

# POLITICS AND GOVERNMENT

The governor of Oregon serves as head of the executive branch of government and is elected to a four-year term. The Legislature is composed of sixty members of the House of Representatives, each serving a two-year term, and thirty members of the Senate, each serving a four-year term.

The highest court in Oregon is the Supreme Court, which is made up of seven elected justices, each serving six-year terms. Oregon's judicial system has municipal, justice, district, and county courts, as well as the court of appeals.

Cities and counties in Oregon can form their own government under a system called "home rule," with a mayor or manager and a city council. Only seven of Oregon's thirty-six counties presently have their own system of government.

**Oregon's first two State Capitols were destroyed by fire. The third and most recent Capitol, built in the 1930s, is fireproof.**

The Scandinavian Festival, in Junction City, attracts visitors from around the country.

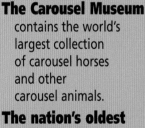
# CULTURAL GROUPS

Junction City pays homage each year to the cultures of Denmark, Finland, Norway, Sweden, and Iceland with the Scandinavian Festival. Entertainment, activities, and displays of old-world crafts are part of the celebration. During the four-day festival in August, the entire downtown of Junction City is transformed into an old-fashioned Scandinavian town. Popular events include folk dancing and storytelling.

At the Tsalila Festival, the Confederated Tribes of Coos, Lower Umpqua, and Siuslaw honor their heritage with dancing, drumming, traditional crafts, and an alder-smoked salmon dinner. The festival takes place each year along the Umpqua riverfront in Reedsport, Oregon, as part of the Umpqua River Festival.

The Junction City Scandinavian Festival has been held every year since 1961.

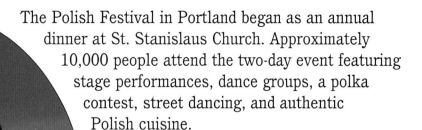

The Polish Festival in Portland began as an annual dinner at St. Stanislaus Church. Approximately 10,000 people attend the two-day event featuring stage performances, dance groups, a polka contest, street dancing, and authentic Polish cuisine.

Oregon's agricultural heritage is celebrated in such events as Sutherlin's Annual Blackberry Festival, featuring blackberry cook-offs, craft and food booths, bog races, mud volleyball, and lawn mower races.

The Flock and Fiber Festival, in Canby, celebrates the region's sheep-raising and wool-processing industries. The festival features a sheep show, with top sheep taking home prizes in different categories. A variety of wool garments and art are on display throughout the festival.

**When Russia sold Alaska to the United States, many Russians who were living there chose to move to Oregon, rather than return to Russia.**

## QUICK FACTS

**Woodburn is home** to a community of Russian Old Believers, who split from the Russian Church in the 1660s. The community maintains their traditional dress, religion, and culture.

**The first African** American to step foot on Oregon soil was Marcus Lopez, a member of Robert Gray's crew in 1788.

**Portland holds a** juggling festival every year.

**Portland's Chinatown is** a celebration of 135 years of Chinese history in Oregon.

**The twin lions at the entrance to Portland's Chinatown are well-known landmarks.**

**The Simpsons is the longest running cartoon in television history.**

# ARTS AND ENTERTAINMENT

Cultural and artistic life is centered around Oregon's largest cities and fine educational institutions, such as Oregon State University at Corvallis and the University of Oregon at Eugene. Symphony orchestras, ballet and modern dance companies, choirs, and theatrical companies are found in Portland, Eugene, and Salem. The state's writers and artists have contributed greatly to Oregon's reputation in the arts, as have some major annual entertainment events.

Ashland is home to the Oregon Shakespeare Festival. Founded in 1935 as part of Independence Day celebrations, the festival has grown to become one of the most respected Shakespearian troupes in the country. Every year, from February through October, the company performs five of Shakespeare's plays and six plays by other well-known playwrights.

## QUICK FACTS

**Matt Groening,** creator of *The Simpsons*, was born in Portland.

**Jane Powell,** actress and singer, was born in Portland. Powell's roles in Hollywood musicals of the Golden Era earned her the nickname "Everyone's Favorite Little Sister."

**Oregon's finest female** poet, Hazel Hall, was honored with a memorial in 2000 by the Oregon Cultural Heritage Commission. Hall died in 1924 at the age of 38 years.

**The Oregon Country Fair,** in Eugene, is held annually in July. Food and craft booths sell handmade products from across the state.

**The Oregon Country Fair began as a school fund-raiser more than 30 years ago.**

**Author Ken Kesey attended the University of Oregon.**

Charles Heiden, the founder and conductor of the Salem Symphony, founded the Haydn Festival in 1979, which has transformed over the years to become the Oregon Coast Music Festival. Every summer, symphony orchestras, regional choirs, and chamber groups take part in the three-week festival. In addition to classical music, the festival has recently begun to offer jazz, bluegrass, and world music as part of its annual program.

Some of the country's most celebrated authors have come from Oregon. John Reed, the author of *Ten Days That Shook the World*, was born in Portland in 1887. His book was a first-person account of the Russian revolution in 1917. Many modern journalists have been influenced by his style. Raymond Carver was the author of numerous short stories and collections of poetry. He was born in Clatskanie in 1938. His short stories have been praised as some of the best literature from the United States in the late twentieth century. Ken Kesey, the author of *One Flew Over the Cuckoo's Nest*, was raised in Oregon.

## QUICK FACTS

**Doc Severinsen,** the band leader and principal trumpeter for *The Tonight Show starring Johnny Carson*, was born in Arlington, Oregon.

**Sally Struthers,** who performed as Gloria on Norman Lear's groundbreaking television comedy, *All in the Family*, was born in Portland.

**Other great** Oregon music festivals include the Oregon Bach Festival, the North by Northwest Music Conference and Festival, the Oregon Festival of American Music, and the Southcoast Dixieland Clambake Jazz Festival.

**Television actor Sally Struthers has won two Emmy Awards. She also devotes her time and energy to charity work.**

# SPORTS

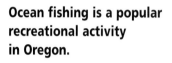

Ocean fishing is a popular recreational activity in Oregon.

Basketball fans in Oregon follow the Portland Trail Blazers, a National Basketball Association (NBA) team that regularly competes in the championship playoffs. The team was formed in 1970 and in just 7 years moved from being one of the worst teams in basketball to one of the best. The 1976–1977 season created the phenomenon Oregonians know as "Blazermania." April 1977 was the last time a Portland fan could just walk up to the ticket booth before a game and buy a ticket. Every one of the nearly 13,000 seats in Memorial Coliseum was sold out for home games from that date until the mid-1990s.

The Blazers went on to numerous playoffs over the years but never repeated their 1977 championship highlight. Top performers, such as Clyde Drexler, Kevin Duckworth, Terry Porter, Cliff Robinson, Chris Dudley, Otis Thorpe, Damon Stoudamire, and Brian Grant, have kept Blazermania alive for more than two decades.

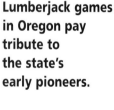

Lumberjack games in Oregon pay tribute to the state's early pioneers.

**Recreational fishers in Oregon can fish for salmon, sturgeon, steelhead, walleye, and shad.**

Portland also hosts women's professional basketball in the form of the Portland Fire. A new team, the Fire have enjoyed success in their first season and are rapidly acquiring a base of loyal fans.

In addition to these two major professional teams, Oregonians enjoy watching the Portland Winter Hawks, a Western Hockey League team that plays in the Rose Quarter complex in Portland; the Portland Beavers, a Triple-A baseball team; and the Eugene Emeralds and the Salem-Keizer Volcanoes, which are Single-A baseball teams.

University and college teams enjoy a loyal following as well. The Oregon Ducks in Eugene, the Oregon State Beavers at Corvallis, the Pacific Boxers in Forest Grove, and the Willamette Bearcats in Salem are all outstanding entertainment.

## QUICK FACTS

**Eugene was voted** one of the top ten bicycling communities in the country by *Bicycling* magazine.

**Dave Kingman,** a major-league baseball player born in Pendleton, hit 442 home runs over his professional career in the 1970s and 1980s.

**Steve Prefontaine was** a phenomenal track athlete whose life was cut tragically short at the age of 24. He is honored every year with a memorial run in his hometown of Coos Bay.

**Timberline Lodge Ski Area,** at Mount Hood, is the only North-American ski resort with year-round skiing.

**Track athlete** Joni Huntley, was born in McMinnville.

**White-water rafting in Oregon is the perfect outdoor adventure. Trips range from half-day rides to five-day camping excursions.**

# Brain Teasers

## 1

How tall is Oregon's tallest tree?

a. 293 feet

b. 329 feet

c. 392 feet

d. 932 feet

Answer: b. Oregon's tallest tree, a Douglas fir, was measured at 329 feet.

## 2

True or False?

The border between Oregon and California was established in a treaty between the United States and Spain.

Answer: True. The treaty was signed in 1819.

## 3

True or False?

Oregon is the only state that has an official state nut.

Answer: True. Oregon's official state nut is the hazelnut.

## 4

The first city to have one-way streets was:

a. Eugene

b. Salem

c. Portland

d. Arlington

Answer: a. Eugene was the first city in Oregon to have one-way streets.

**5**

**How tall is Haystack Rock?**

a. 102 feet

b. 201 feet

c. 235 feet

d. 325 feet

**Answer: c.** Haystack Rock is over 235 feet tall and is considered one of the largest free-standing rocks in the world.

**6**

**True or False?**

**The Capitol of Oregon used to be in Portland.**

**Answer:** False. Before Salem was chosen as the capital, Oregon City and Corvallis were each state capitals.

**7**

**True or False?**

**Tillamook Rock Lighthouse is now used as a cemetery.**

**Answer: True.** The lighthouse was turned into a cemetery in 1980.

**8**

**Which city in Oregon has a volcano within its city limits?**

**Answer:** Portland. The city's Mount Tabor Park is home to an extinct volcano.

# FOR MORE INFORMATION

## Books

Aukshunas, Jane and Karl Samson. *Frommer's Oregon*. New York: Hungry Minds, Inc., 2000.

Cronon, William and William G. Robbins. *Landscapes of Promise: The Oregon Story 1800-1940*. Seattle: University of Washington Press, 1997.

Trinklein, Michael. *Fantastic Facts about the Oregon Trail*. Pocatello, ID: Boettcher/Trinklein, 1995.

## Web Sites

You can also go online and have a look at the following Web sites:

Oregon OnLine
http://www.state.or.us

50 States: Oregon
http://www.50states.com/oregon.htm

Oregon: Just 4 Kids
http://www.econ.state.or.us/kidrptf.htm

Some Web sites stay current longer than others. To find other Oregon Web sites, enter search terms such as "Oregon," "Portland," "Pacific Northwest," or any other topic you want to research.

# GLOSSARY

**biotechnology:** the use of living organisms in technology

**board feet:** a unit of measurement for lumber, equal to 1 inch thick by 1 foot wide by 1 foot long

**Continental Divide:** an imaginary line along the Rocky Mountains that separates those rivers that flow west to the Pacific Ocean and those that flow east to the Atlantic Ocean

**gross state product:** the value in dollars of goods and services produced in the state in one year

**Hudson's Bay Company:** a North American fur-trading company established in 1670

**hydroelectricity:** energy created from moving water

**Louisiana Purchase:** a large amount of territory west of the Mississippi River purchased from France by the United States in 1803

**migration:** a movement of people from one place to another

**nickel:** a hard, silvery metal used in alloys

**Northwest Passage:** an ice-free waterway from the Atlantic Ocean to the Pacific Ocean

# INDEX